NINJAK

THE FIST & THE STEEL

MATT KINDT | KHARI EVANS | ANDRÉS GUINALDO | ULISES ARREOLA

CONTENTS

Collection Cover Art: Diego Latorre

Assistant Editors: Danny Khazem (#18-20) and Lauren Hitzhusen (#19)
Editor: Kyle Andrukiewicz
Editor-in-Chief: Warren Simons

VALIANT

Ninjak®: The Fist & The Steel. Published by Valiant Entertainment LLC. Office of Publication: 350 Seventh Avenue, New York, NY 10001. Compilation copyright © 2017 Valiant Entertainment LLC. All rights reserved. Contains materials originally published in single magazine form as Ninjak #18-21. Copyright © 2016 Valiant Entertainment LLC. All rights reserved. All characters, their distinctive likeness and related indicia featured in this publication are trademarks of Valiant Entertainment LLC. The stories, characters, and incidents featured in this publication are entirely fictional. Valiant Entertainment does not read or accept unsolicited submissions of ideas, stories, or artwork. Printed in the U.S.A. First Printing. ISBN: 9781682151792.

MATT KINDT
KHARI EVANS
RES GUINALDO
JSES ARREOLA
IS SOTOMAYOR
NINJAK
VALIANT
#18
PART 1
THE FIST & THE STEEL

is name is Ninjak, spy and mercenary for hire. He is also Colin King, a once wealthy son of privilege. He works for
ighest bidder, though his conscience often aligns him with the good guys. He is an expert in combat and espionage.
as ruthless as he is charming. He is...

NINJAK®

Ninjak has been run ragged by the deadly Roku, who systematically destroyed Ninjak's life--his home, his contacts, his relationships. But resilient as always, Ninjak defeated Roku and must now rebuild.

But not everyone has abandoned Colin. In fact, despite their differences, the Eternal Warrior will remain

YOUR HEAD OKAY?
YES. YES. JUST A SPOT OF JET LAG.
AS I WAS SAYING...NEXT TIME THE GEOMANCER'S IN TROUBLE, YOU DON'T HAVE TO GO IT ALONE.

MANY YEARS FROM NOW.
I AM THE FIST AND STEEL, COLIN. IT IS MY SWORN DUTY TO *PROTECT* THE *PROTECTOR* OF EARTH. THE GEOMANCER--
I KNOW, GILAD. I'M NOT SAYING THAT'S *NOT* YOUR DUTY. IF I'VE LEARNED ONE THING OVER THE YEARS, IT'S THIS-- COLLABORATION ISN'T ALWAYS A BAD THING.
LOOK AT US NOW? WORKING TOGETHER. GETTING ALONG.
I WOULDN'T SAY THAT.
MI-6X ASKED ME TO TRACK DOWN ONE OF THEIR ESCAPED PRISONERS. SOMEONE YOU CAPTURED YEARS AGO.

AND I'M MORE THAN HAPPY TO HELP. IT'S BLOODY DAMN TIME MI-6X LET BYGONES BE BYGONES AND HIRED ME AGAIN.
...
WHAT?
MI-6X DOESN'T KNOW YOU CONTACTED ME DO THEY?
YOU'RE ON THE "DO-NOT-CONTACT" LIST.
STILL? BLIMEY. WHAT DOES A BLOKE HAVE TO DO? IT'S BEEN THREE YEARS SINCE--
SINCE YOU LEAKED THE BUCKINGHAM PALACE PAPERS.
LISTEN. IT WAS THE ONLY WAY TO GET RID OF THE ENTIRE CORRUPT LOT OF AGENTS THAT HAD INFILTRATED THE BRITISH SECRET SERVICE.
YOU SINGLE-HANDEDLY DESTROYED MI-6.

IT'S DEFINITELY MORE NUANCED THAN THAT. BUT WHAT CAN I EXPECT FROM YOU? I THINK YOU'VE PROBABLY DIED ONE TOO MANY TIMES.
YOU SURE ALL YOUR GREY MATTER IS IMMORTAL?
YOU SHOULD NOT TALK ABOUT MATTERS YOU DON'T FULLY UNDERSTAND.
SCANNING...
YOU'RE NOT SCANNING ME ARE YOU?
NO. WHY?
YOU ASKED ME TO HELP. SO I'M HELPING.
BUT WE'RE GOING TO DO IT *MY WAY*.
QUICK. QUIET. SUBTLE. OKAY?
YOU ALWAYS SAY THAT.

YOU WANT TO FIND OUT WHERE YOUR ESCAPED PRISONER IS? WELL, HIS AGENT IS IN THE NEXT CAR--COMPLETELY OBLIVIOUS TO OUR PRESENCE. WE CATCH HIM BY SURPRISE, WE MAKE IT QUICK, AND WE EXTRACT OUR INFO. IN AND OUT.
WAIT FOR MY SIGNAL. I MAY NOT EVEN NEED YOU.

FACIAL RECOGNITION SHOULD PICK UP OUR POTENTIAL INFORMANT. GUY NAMED FITZ.
MASTER-LEVEL SKILLS IN EVERY KNOWN FORM OF COMBAT. TOUGH LITTLE GIT BUT NOTHING I CAN'T HANDLE.
I HAVE EYES ON TARGET...
CONFIRMED. THIS IS OUR GUY. HE SHOULD BE ABLE TO TELL US WHERE YOUR MISSING CONVICT IS.
HOLD ON...
MULTIPLE TARGETS...

FACIAL RECOGNITION IS GOING CRAZY...
THEY'RE ALL FITZ...
...A LOT OF THEM.
BLOODY HELL. OF COURSE A CLONE WOULDN'T GO SOLO.
HOLD OFF GILAD. I'VE GOT THIS. A LITTLE NERVE GAS SHOULD KNOCK THEM ALL--
KABOOOOM!!

IF I WAITED FOR YOU TO HANDLE THINGS...
BUDDA BUDDA BUDDA BUDDA
...WE'D STILL BE CLEANING UP THE NANITES IN MOSCOW.
BUDDA BUDDA BUDDA BUDDA
KA-SHUKKK!

BUDDA
BUDDABUDDA
BUDDA
KRUNCH
K-RRASSSHH!
SHUKK
BUDDA
BUDDA
BUDDA
BUDDA
BUDDA
BUDDA
BUDDA
BUDDA

SHUNK
KRUKK
FWUMP
KA-BOOOOOM!
WHAT ARE YOU DOING?
FWUMP
FACIAL RECOGNITION PULLED YOU OUT OF THE CROWD. YOU'RE DIFFERENT. WHAT'S YOUR STORY?
LOOK, DUDE. I KNOW WHY YOU'RE HERE AND I DON'T WANT ANY PART OF THIS. I WAS JUST WAITING FOR MY OPPORTUNITY TO OFF ALL OF THESE FOOLS.
BUT YOU KNOW HOW HARD IT IS TO KILL TWENTY CLONES OF YOURSELF, ALL TRAINED EXPERTS IN HUNDREDS OF FIGHTING STYLES? *IT AIN'T EASY.*
I DON'T KNOW THE EXACT COORDINATES. BUT I CAN TELL YOU THE GUY YOU'RE LOOKING FOR IS...

"...SOMEWHERE IN THE HIMALAYAS."
HE SAYS "SOMEWHERE IN THE HIMALAYAS" AND YOU LET HIM LIVE? NO TORTURE TO GET EXACT COORDINATES? HE HAD TO KNOW MORE. WHY'D YOU TRUST HIM?
I *KNOW* WHERE FAKIR IS.
RIGHT. WHICH IS WHY YOU'VE HAD US WANDERING FOR HALF A DAY LIKE YOU FORGOT WHERE YOU PARKED YOUR CAR.
HOLD ON I--
NGH
YOU OKAY?
YEAH. IT'S OKAY. JUST AN OLD...AN OLD INJURY.
DON'T WORRY. THIS IS WHERE I TRAINED MANY YEARS AGO. IT'S A TRICKY PLACE TO FIND BUT WE'RE CLOSE.
THE QUESTION IS...

"...WHAT IS FAKIR DOING BACK HERE?"
YOU MUST WORK METICULOUSLY!
WE ARE IN SEARCH OF EVERY PARTICLE! EVERY DEAD SKIN CELL!
ANY REMNANT, ANY TISSUE OR DNA, NO MATTER HOW MINISCULE, MUST BE RETRIEVED...
...IF WE ARE TO BRING THE UNDEAD MONK BACK TO LIFE!

BEEP BEEP!
BEEP BEEP!
YES?
WHAT? NO, NO. EVERYTHING'S FINE. WHY DO YOU ASK?
THE RECOVERY IS GOING AS PLANNED. THERE ARE ONLY SEVEN PEOPLE ON EARTH WHO COULD EVEN FIND THIS PLACE AGAIN AND AS FAR AS I NOW THERE ARE ONLY TWO OF STILL AROUND.

HE'S JUST DOWN THERE IN THE VALLEY.
EVEN WITH ALL MY ARMOR, I'M STILL FREEZING MY ASS OFF!
I'M HALF-BURIED IN THE MIDDLE OF A BLIZZARD. I CAN'T SEE A THING!
PERHAPS WE SHOULD CALL IN UNITY OR JUST LET ME GO IN AS A DECOY AND FLUSH THEM OUT--
NO. THIS TIME WE DO IT THE *EASY* WAY.
YOU REALIZE YOU SAY THAT *EVERY TIME* WE'RE ABOUT TO ENTER BATTLE.
BIO-BALLS WILL DO THE TRICK. TARGETS ANY DNA I PROGRAM INTO IT. SHOULD TAKE OUT ANY MORE OF THOSE CLONES IF THEY'RE HERE.
I WORRY YOU RELY TO MUCH ON YOUR TECHNOLOGY, COLIN...
YOU SAY *THAT* EVERY TIME, GILAD. PROBLEM IS, IF ALL YOU HAVE IS AN AXE...

"...EVERY PROBLEM LOOKS LIKE A TREE."
I CAN'T HELP IT IF YOUR CLONES CAN'T KEEP THEIR MOUTHS SHUT.
YES, YES. WE'RE GOING OVER EVERY INCH.
WE'RE COLLECTING *EVERYTHING*. WHEN I'M DONE, I'LL POP INTO THE PORTAL, DELIVER YOUR "CALAMITY PARTICLES" AND OUR BUSINESS WILL BE CONCLUDED. TRUST ME, I WANT THIS OVER...
BOOM!
BOOM!
...AS QUICKLY AS POSSIBLE...?
BOOM!
BOOM!

UH...LET ME CALL YOU BACK.
WHO IS IT?
WHO'S THERE?!
CAN'T SEE A DAMN THING...

WE TRAINED TOGETHER, HERE, FAKIR. DO YOU REMEMBER?
WE WERE BOTH STUDENTS OF THE *UNDEAD MONK.*
YOU WENT ON TO DO SOME BLOODY AWFUL THINGS.
BUT IT'S NOT TOO LATE.
WHO IS THAT? ROKU? NOT KANNON... HE'S GONE. THAT ONLY LEAVES...

QUIT WHILE YOU'RE AHEAD AND I WON'T KILL YOU.

NINJAK!
I TOOK SOME OF THOSE ARMS OFF BEFORE. DON'T MAKE ME DO IT AGAIN.
THEY GROW BACK.
YOU DON'T KNOW WHAT YOU'RE DEALING WITH!
WHO YOU'RE DEALING WITH!
IF THAT'S HOW IT'S GOING TO BE...
SWHIK!
I'M GETTING OLD, FAKIR.

SHIKK
DON'T ENJOY A GOOD JOG LIKE I USED TO.
KA-CHIKK
HUFF! HUFF!
HUFF! HUFF!
FWISSHH!

...APERIESQUE OSTIUM...
FWUNK!
NOW WHAT?
I THINK... WE FOLLOW HIM.

AFTER YOU.
TO BE CONTINUED...

KING'S CASTLE, ENGLAND.
PRESENT DAY.
THE LOST FILES
IT COULD BE WORSE, COLIN.

NEVILLE. WHAT ARE YOU DOING HERE?
LETTING YOU KNOW THAT IT COULD BE WORSE.
YOU HAVE NO IDEA WHAT YOU'RE TALKING ABOUT. NO IDEA THE LENGTHS THAT ROKU WENT TO DESTROY MY LIFE.
SHE TOOK EVERYTHING. MY MONEY. MY... PARENTS.
ANGELINA. SHE SAID SHE *WAS* ANGELINA. SO SHE TOOK THAT MEMORY, TOO.
I *LOVED* ANGELINA. ROKU IS *NOT* HER.

...
WELL. I'M ON "ADMINISTRATIVE LEAVE." WHICH MAKES IMMENSELY MORE TIME FOR ME TO SEE MY EX-WIFE AND KID. BUT THEY WON'T TALK TO ME...
...BECAUSE I'VE SPENT THE BETTER PART OF THESE LAST FEW YEARS WITH YOU. HELPING YOU. PROTECTING YOU.
I WAS SO FAR OUT OF TOUCH. SO DEEP INTO WORK. *OUR* WORK...I DIDN'T EVEN REALIZE I'D LOST VISITATION RIGHTS UNTIL I WAS FIRED.
...

YOUR FLAT BLOW UP?
NO. YOU HAVE ONE-UPPED ME ON THAT FRONT. AND MI-6 HAS GIVEN ME PAID LEAVE. I CAN AFFORD LUNCH.
LET ME TREAT YOU? LUNCH. OR A PINT?
NO, THANKS. I'M DONE, NEVILLE. WITH MI-6. AND YOU. I'M FREELANCE. I ALWAYS WAS. ME AND YOU AND MI-6 WAS A CONVENIENT ARRANGEMENT. BUT I WORK BETTER ALONE.
OBVIOUSLY.
THIS IS ON YOU, NEVILLE. ON MI-6. YOU SENT ME AFTER ROKU EARLY ON. YOU SHOULD HAVE KNOWN WHAT SHE WAS. WHAT SHE WAS PART OF.

I CAN'T TRUST YOU. THAT'S THE SHORT OF IT.
YOU WERE THE ONLY AGENT THAT COULD HAVE LEAKED MY FILES.
AS FAR AS I'M CONCERNED, THE NEXT MI-6 AGENT THAT SHOWS UP ON MY DOORSTEP WILL LEAVE HERE WITH A SWORD IN THEM.
INCLUDING *YOU.*
COLIN...
I KNOW ALL THIS...BUT THAT'S NOT WHY I'M REALLY HERE.

THERE'S SOMETHING ELSE GOING ON. SOMETHING... BAD.
THE NINETEEN MI-6 OPERATIVES YOU SAVED FROM THE DEADSIDE? PUNK MAMBO'S TASK FORCE? THEY'RE DYING. SLOWLY. PAINFULLY. I DOWNLOADED THEIR RECORDS RIGHT BEFORE I WAS FIRED.
THEY'VE GOT SOME KIND OF...I DON'T KNOW. A SICKNESS FROM THE DEADSIDE.
"TURNS OUT YOU WERE RIGHT TO BE A LITTLE MENTAL ABOUT GERMS OVER THERE.
"SYMPTOMS ARE...EXTREME. INTENSE PAIN. PSYCHOSIS... IT'S NOT GOOD."
IT'S AN AGGRESSIVE BRAIN TUMOR. NOT CANCER. SOMETHING...ELSE. SOMETHING UNIQUE TO THE DEADSIDE. I HESITATE TO CALL IT "MAGIC," BUT OUR MEDICAL TEAM CAN'T FIGURE IT OUT.

ALSO THOUGHT I WOULD GIVE YOU A HEADS UP...JUST IN CASE...
IN CASE YOU'RE INFECTED, TOO.
I'M DONE, NEVILLE. I TOLD YOU. NO MORE MI-6. NO MORE YOU. I'M TIGHTENING MY CIRCLE. I WON'T BE BURNED AGAIN.
OKAY. WELL. THOUGHT I'D REACH OUT. AS ONE MATE... TO ANOTHER.
ANYWAY. THEY'RE DYING. THOUGHT MAYBE YOU MIGHT WANT TO HELP. SEE IF YOU HAD ANY IDEAS FOR HOW TO TREAT IT. MAYBE ONE MORE MISSION TO THE DEADSIDE TO FIND A CURE?
CHEERS.

NGH!
...NGGHH...
GAHHHH!
TO BE CONTINUED...

MATT KINDT
KHARI EVANS
RES GUINALDO
LISES ARREOLA
RIS SOTOMAYOR
VALIANT
#19
NINJAK
THE FIST & THE STEEL

NGH. HEAD IS KILLING ME.
YOU GOING TO BE OKAY, COLIN?
GILAD. IT'S YOUR FAULT.
HOW IS IT MY FAULT?
YOU CALLED ME ON THIS MISSION, KNOWING FULL WELL THAT MI-6X DIDN'T SANCTION ME.
YOU HAD SOME FAMILIARITY WITH MY TARGET-- THE FAKIR. YOU TANGLED WITH HIM IN THE PAST. THOUGHT YOU MIGHT BE OF USE.
YOU AGREED TO HELP. I ONLY REQUESTED YOUR INTEL. YOU'RE FREE TO LEAVE ANY TIME YOU WANT.
I WASN'T THE ONE THAT MADE YOU JUMP INTO THE MYSTERY PORTAL... AND INTO...

...WHATEVER WE'RE IN NOW.
OUR TARGET'S INJURED. HE JUMPED IN THIS PORTAL. WE *HAD* TO FOLLOW HIM.
DID YOU SEE--?
FOCUS, GILAD. I'VE BEEN THROUGH PORTALS LIKE THIS BEFORE. YOU GET SIDETRACKED, YOU *DIE.*
THIS ONE SEEMS TO BE A KIND OF WORMHOLE THAT USES THE DEADSIDE CURRENT TO--

JUST FIND THE EXIT.
UH. FOUND IT.
YOU'RE KIDDING.
YOU WANT TO FIND YOUR MISSING PRISONER AND RETURN HIM TO MI-6X?
ARE YOU JUST NOT SEEING ALL THIS?!
SIGH...
COLIN-- OOF--WHERE ARE WE?
EGYPT... BUT NOT QUITE RIGHT...
I DON'T THINK WE FELL BACK IN TIME, GILAD.

LAS VEGAS, NEVADA.
WE JUST STEPPED ACROSS THE GLOBE.

JUST FOLLOW MY LEAD. THE KEY TO ESPIONAGE IS TO JUST FIT IN. *BLEND.*
AND IF YOU CAN'T BLEND IN... JUST ACT LIKE YOU'RE SUPPOSED TO BE HERE.
NEED A ROOM FOR THE NIGHT. TWO BEDS IF YOU DON'T MIND.
OKAY. LET ME SEE WHAT WE HAVE. LOOKS LIKE YOU TWO ARE IN TOWN FOR THE SHOW SO I CAN GIVE YOU THE SHOW RATE...
WE'LL TAKE THE BEST YOU HAVE. PENTHOUSE IF IT'S AVAILABLE. A SUITE AT THE VERY LEAST.
I'LL DO WHAT I CAN SIR, BUT WITHOUT A RESERVATION I'M AFRAID YOU'LL HAVE TO TAKE WHAT IS AVAILABLE.
OF COURSE. HE'S JUST A VERY HEAVY SNORER. DOOR-RATTLING SINUSES. HATE TO BOTHER THE OTHER GUESTS.
OOOKAY.

SO WHAT'S OUR MOVE?
WHOEVER OPENED THE PORTAL ON TOP OF THE PYRAMID HERE IN VEGAS PROBABLY OWNS THE PROPERTY IT'S ON.
SHOULDN'T BE HARD TO TRACK DOWN. WE JUST HEAD TO THE REAL ESTATE OFFICE AND SEARCH--
KNOCK KNOCK!
YOU EXPECTING SOMEONE?

TAKE IT EASY. LET ME DO THE TALKING.
EXCUSE ME, SIR. THE SUITS YOU ORDERED...?
OH, YES. OF COURSE. THANK YOU, WILLIAM.
I'VE WIRED A THOUSAND DOLLARS TO YOUR ACCOUNT, AS USUAL. WE'D...APPRECIATE YOUR DISCRETION.
CERTAINLY, SIR.
READY TO GO UNDERCOVER?

THE REAL ESTATE AGENCY ITSELF IS OFFLINE. IMPOSSIBLE TO HACK. MY INTEL SAYS THIS IS WHERE THE OFFICE IS LOCATED. BUT NOW THAT I SEE THE PLACE...
...I'M QUESTIONING MY INTEL.
SOMETIMES I THINK YOU DO THINGS LIKE THIS ON PURPOSE.
YOU FELLAS TAKE A WRONG TURN? I THINK THE BAR YOU WANT'S ACROSS THE STREET.

LOOKING FOR THE PROPRIETOR OF *UNREAL ESTATE INCORPORATED.* ANYBODY SEEN THE BOSS?
WHO THE #*$@ IS ASKING?
WELL. SINCE YOU ASKED...
I'M STEEL. BEHIND ME IS MY ASSOCIATE. HE CALLS HIMSELF "FIST."
YOU TELL US WHAT WE NEED TO KNOW? YOU WON'T GET BOTH.
BOTH WHAT?
THE FIST...
...AND THE STEEL.

GET THEM!
SHKR
KRNCH
FWIP
FWIP
SHK
SHK
WHMP!
WOULD YOU CARE TO JOIN YOUR ASSOCIATES OR...?
OHHHH...
...AHHHG...
--U-UP STAIRS...!

"KEY TO ESPIONAGE IS TO FIT IN..."
THAT IS ABSOLUTELY THE LAST SUIT I EVER BUY YOU.
WARRIORS DON'T WEAR SUITS.
SHOULD WE KNOCK OR--
KERRANNCH
BOYS! HOW MANY TIMES HAVE I TOLD YOU...

KEEP THE FIGHTING DOWNSTAIRS. THIS IS MY OFFICE. MY *SANCTUM SOLITARY.*
THE BUFFER BETWEEN ME AND--OH!
I DON'T KNOW YOU. YOU KNOW YOU'RE GOING TO HAVE TO PAY FOR THAT DOOR.
THAT WON'T BE A PROBLEM.
NOW, WE'RE LOOKING FOR INFORMATION ON THE OWNER OF THE PYRAMID CASINO IN THE CENTER OF TOWN.
DOES... YOUR PARTNER ALWAYS SMELL LIKE THAT?
JUST A NAME WILL DO. THEN WE'RE OUT OF YOUR HAIR.
...SIGH... I HAVE A LOT OF...*TROUBLESOME* CLIENTS. BUT HE IS HONESTLY THE WORST. MYSTERIOUS "AGENTS" ARE ALWAYS AFTER HIM. HE LIVES JUST OUTSIDE OF THE CITY IN THE DESERT. YOU CAN'T MISS THE PLACE. HE'S AN OLD GUY...

"...GOES BY THE NAME OF SILK."
HOPE THIS IS OUR SILK.
HOW MANY SILKS DO YOU KNOW, GILAD?
ACTUALLY... QUITE A FEW. YOU LIVE AS LONG AS I HAVE, YOU'D BE SURPRISED--
PLEASE, GOD. NOT ANOTHER ONE OF YOUR STORIES.
WELL, SHE WAS RIGHT WHEN SHE SAID WE COULDN'T MISS IT.

THERE'S NO MISSING THAT.
WHAT IS IT WITH THE PYRAMIDS?
THE ARCHITECTURE OF THE PYRAMID ACTUALLY PRE-DATES RECORDED HISTORY. TAPPING INTO--
GILAD.
INTERESTING... SPONTANEOUS ENERGY SPHERE... NO DISCERNABLE SOURCE...
...AND APPARENTLY JUST FOR SHOW.
WHAT IN SODDING HELL IS GOING ON HERE?
WELL, YOU CAN REST ASSURED...

IT DOESN'T INVOLVE THE WORLD'S LOUDEST NINJA AND HIS RUSTY SIDEKICK.
THOUGHT I LOST YOU TWO AT THE HOTEL. MAYBE YOU'RE NOT AS DUMB AS YOU LOOK.
FAKIR. SURPRISED YOU'RE STILL WALKING AROUND AFTER I TOOK ONE OF YOUR HANDS AND PUT AN ARROW IN YOU.
I'VE GOTTEN PRETTY HANDY AT PROTECTING MYSELF, NINJAK.
I'VE GOT HANDS TO SPARE.
TOO MANY...! FOR EVERY ONE I CUT...
...TWO MORE APPEAR...! A LITTLE HELP?

GHKKK!
I GOT YOU.
...GAKK... BREATHE...
WE KNOW SILK IS BEHIND WHATEVER'S GOING ON HERE.
...GHK...
I KNOW HE'S HERE.
GHKKK...
SHHHHHH. QUIET NOW.
YOU TWO CERTAINLY KNOW HOW TO MAKE AN ENTRANCE.
GHKZZZZZZZZ

BUT WHAT COULD YOU TWO STRAPPING YOUNG MEN WANT WITH AN OLD FOSSIL LIKE ME?
BUT I'M BEING RUDE. I SHOULD-- NNFF-- STAND WHEN WELCOMING GUESTS.
YOU REMEMBER THIS, NINJAK? THE UNDEAD MONK I BELIEVE?

I'VE BEEN PAINSTAKINGLY RECOVERING EVERY LAST ONE OF HIS SKIN CELLS OVER THE YEARS.
HE TRAINED YOU, DID HE NOT? A MASTER OF ALL THE DARK MYSTIC ARTS.
HIS... REMNANTS... ALSO HAPPENED TO BE AN EXCELLENT NATURAL RESOURCE TO TAP INTO THE DARK MAGICS.
IMMORTALITY THROUGH SCIENCE HAS FAILED ME. BUT WITH MAGIC...?
ANYTHING IS POSSIBLE.

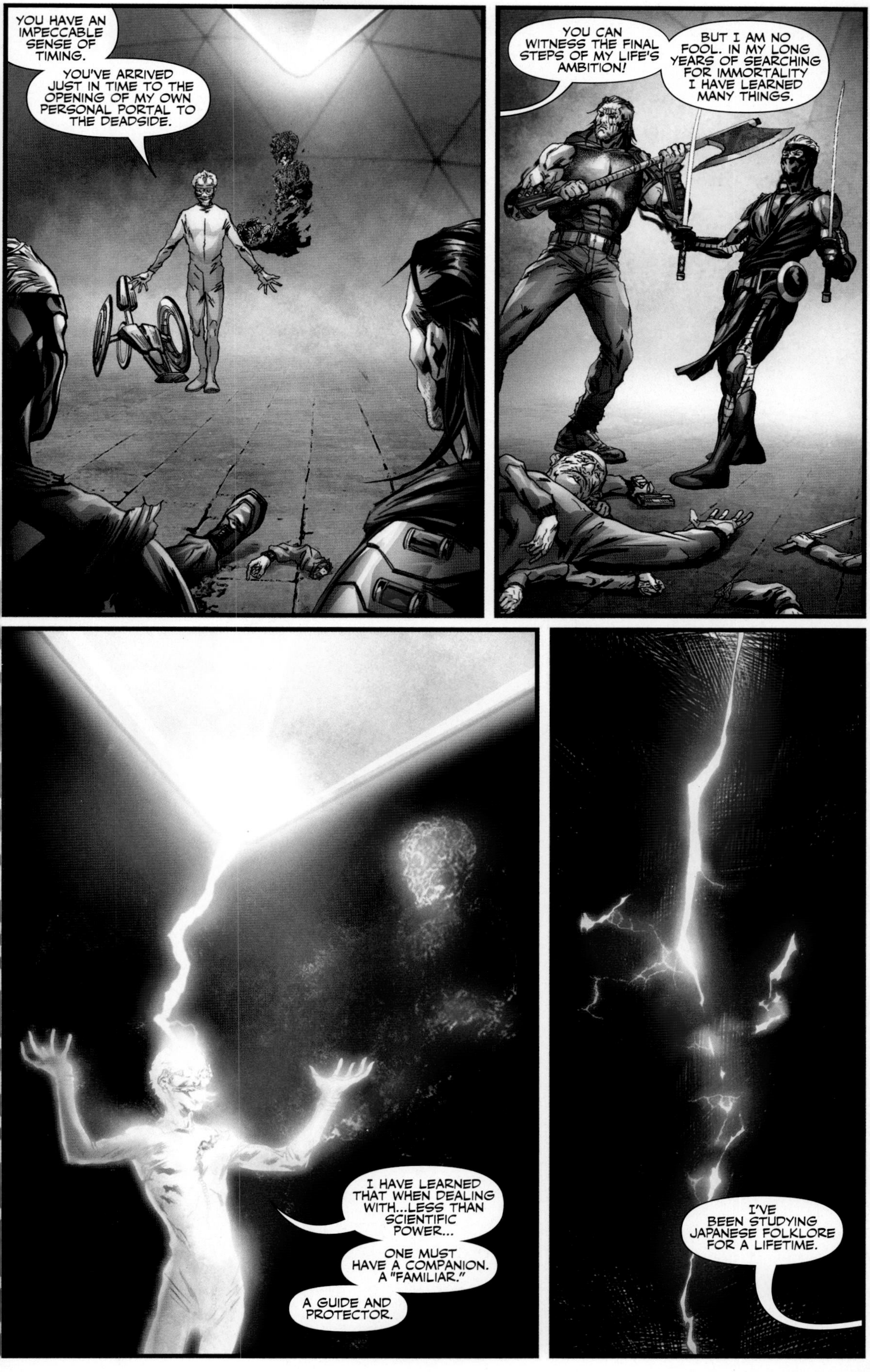
YOU HAVE AN IMPECCABLE SENSE OF TIMING.
YOU'VE ARRIVED JUST IN TIME TO THE OPENING OF MY OWN PERSONAL PORTAL TO THE DEADSIDE.
YOU CAN WITNESS THE FINAL STEPS OF MY LIFE'S AMBITION!
BUT I AM NO FOOL. IN MY LONG YEARS OF SEARCHING FOR IMMORTALITY I HAVE LEARNED MANY THINGS.
I HAVE LEARNED THAT WHEN DEALING WITH...LESS THAN SCIENTIFIC POWER...
ONE MUST HAVE A COMPANION. A "FAMILIAR."
A GUIDE AND PROTECTOR.
I'VE BEEN STUDYING JAPANESE FOLKLORE FOR A LIFETIME.

IT TOOK LIFETIMES OF TRIAL AND ERROR TO GET THE SPELLS CORRECT.
YOU CAN'T IMAGINE THE INACCURACIES IN MAGICAL TEXTS. THE TYPOS AND MISSPELLINGS?
AN EDITOR'S NIGHTMARE. IT'S A WONDER THERE'S ANY MAGIC LEFT IN THE WORLD.
BUT I'VE FINALLY DONE IT.
EVERY CULTURE HAS THEIR OWN POWER SPIRITS.

I FOUND THE JAPANESE CULTURE TO HAVE THE MOST... *PLIABLE* SPIRITS...
AND THE MOST POWERFUL.
SO I FOUND ONE ALL FOR MYSELF, WITH ENOUGH POWER TO MAKE AN OLD MAN...

...FEEL YOUNG AGAIN.
TO BE CONTINUED...

KING'S CASTLE, ENGLAND. PRESENT DAY.
THE LOST FILES
I CAN'T THANK YOU ENOUGH FOR COMING OUT, LIVEWIRE. TRULY ABOVE AND BEYOND.
I'M NOT DOING THIS OUT OF A SENSE OF DUTY, NEVILLE.
NINJAK IS...COLIN IS A FRIEND.

WHAT HAPPENED? WHY...WHY DID YOU LEAVE HIM LIKE THIS?
WELL. TO BE HONEST. WE HAD A BIT OF A ROW.
A FALLING OUT YOU COULD SAY.
AND THEN HE JUST COLLAPSED... AND WENT INTO THIS ZEN THING HERE... AND HE HASN'T MOVED SINCE.
WELL. HE'S BREATHING.
IF I DIDN'T KNOW BETTER, I'D SAY HE'S IN A DEEP MEDITATIVE STATE.
REPAIRING HIMSELF? MAYBE FIGHTING WHATEVER VIRUS HE PICKED UP IN THE DEADSIDE?

LET'S SCAN HIM AND SEE.
WHAT'S THAT THING?
KIND OF LIKE A CAT SCAN...ON STEROIDS. SOMETHING I DEVELOPED. BEEN MAKING THEM AND DONATING TO HOSPITALS.
STILL IN THE EXPERIMENTAL PHASE BUT IT'S DOING WONDERS IN THIRD-WORLD COUNTRIES.
NEARLY DONE...
THERE.

LET'S HAVE A LOOK INSIDE COLIN'S HEAD.
THAT'S STRANGE.
WHAT IS IT?
I... I DON'T KNOW.
SOMETHING THAT...THAT SHOULDN'T BE THERE.
LET ME SEE IF I CAN CLEAN UP THAT IMAGE.

OH MY GOD.
WHAT THE BLOODY HELL? SOMETHING'S IN THERE.
WHAT IS THAT?!
SCANNING THE NET. LET'S SEE...
CLIK
LOOKS LIKE... SOMETHING OLD.
FOUND REFERENCES TO IT IN A LOT OF MYTHS AND FOLKLORE.
SOME INSANE *DEADSIDE* STUFF.

BLOODY HELL.
WHATEVER'S IN THERE, NEVILLE...
IT DOESN'T PLAY BY OUR RULES. I COULD CUT IT OUT. BUT WE MIGHT END UP EXPOSING OURSELVES. OR KILLING COLIN IN THE PROCESS.
I'M NOT SURE ANY OF *OUR* SCIENCE CAN FIX IT.
THIS IS *MAGIC* STUFF. SUPER-NATURAL. NOT MY AREA OF EXPERTISE.
HM. WELL. I GUESS THAT JUST LEAVES THE LAST RESORT.
YOU MIND KEEPING WATCH ON COLIN?

"I'M GOING TO CALL IN A FAVOR FROM AN OLD FRIEND."
KNOCK KNOCK
OPEN UP! I DON'T KNOW THE BLOODY PASSWORD THIS WEEK. HOW ABOUT "MI-6 PROMISES NOT TO KICK YOUR DOOR IN?" WILL THAT DO?
KEEP YER VOICE DOWN, YA STUPID GIT.
CHARMING.
WELL THIS IS A RIGHT BLOODY MESS.
YOU ARE IT, LOVE. AS USUAL...MY LAST RESORT.
I NEED YOUR HELP...

...PUNK MAMBO.
$%#@ YOU.

MATT KINDT
KHARI EVANS
DRES GUINALDO
LISES ARREOLA
RIS SOTOMAYOR
NINJAK
VALIANT
#20
THE FIST & THE STEEL

HAHAA!
I'M OLDER THAN DIRT, BUT YOU KNOW WHAT NEVER GETS OLD?
KICKING YOU TWO AROUND.

MISSION ACCOMPLISHED, GILAD. YOU WERE LOOKING FOR YOUR LOST MI-6X PRISONER?
WELL, HERE HE IS.
LAS VEGAS. YEARS FROM NOW.
YES. NOTHING I HATE MORE THAN A BROBDINGNAGIAN ARACHNID THAT'S BEEN ENSORCELLED.
BROBDINGNAGIAN... SERIOUSLY?
ARE YOU TAKING THE PISS?
WHAT?
YOU CAN'T JUST SAY, "I HATE GIANT MAGIC SPIDERS"?
THIS IS WHERE YOU SAY "RELAX, GILAD--LET ME DO IT MY WAY. I'V GOT NINJA STARS THAT BIO-SCAN AND NEUTRALIZE OVERGROWN ARACHNIDS AND THEIR VILLAINOUS MASTERS."
I TOLD YOU COMING HERE WAS A BAD IDEA.
WE CAN TALK ABOUT IT LATE--

NNGGAH!
OOOF!
ZZSHHK-BASSH!
NGGH!
...TOO FAST...

YOU OKAY?
I'M IMMORTAL.
THEN LET'S GO.

FOLLOW MY LEAD.
TINK
TINK
BOOM!
BOOM!
LET ME TELL YOU SOMETHING.
THIS POWER SPIRIT I CONJURED? IT ISN'T FOR HERE.
GAH! DAMMIT, COLIN!
BOLLOCKS.

IT'S FOR THE DEADSIDE.
MI-6X MAY HAVE A WARRANT FOR MY ARREST, BUT THEY HAVE NO JURISDICTION IN THE DEADSIDE.
WHAT BETTER PLACE TO FIND THE ANSWER TO IMMORTALITY THAN A LAND THAT LIVES ON DEATH?
THUNK! THUNK! THUNK!
I'VE BEEN THERE. AND I'VE DISCOVERED SOMETHING. SOMETHING... *BEAUTIFUL.* THE *DEADSIDE INTELLIGENCE MECHANISM.* CAN YOU IMAGINE?

IT HAS ALL THE ANSWERS TO LIFE AND DEATH--ALL THE SECRETS OF THE UNIVERSE! ULTIMATE KNOWLEDGE! IMMORTALITY!
CURES FOR CANCER? KNOWLEDGE OF THE AFTERLIFE? IT'S WHERE MAGIC AND SCIENCE MEET.
I'M BANISHING MYSELF, BOYS.
AND I'M GETTING A LITTLE TIRED OF YOU DOGGING MY HEELS. GIVE IT A REST, FELLAS.
CONSIDER YOUR WORK DONE. WHERE I'M GOING? BRITISH INTELLIGENCE HAS NO AUTHORITY.

BLOKE'S GOT A POINT. HE STAYS IN THE DEADSIDE, HE'S *DEADSIDE'S* PROBLEM. NOT YOURS, MINE, OR MI-6X'S.
YOU GOING TO BE ABLE TO SLEEP AT NIGHT, KNOWING SILK IS OVER THERE ACCESSING AN OMNIPOTENT MAGICAL COMPUTER?

WANT ME TO GIVE YOU A BOOST OR...?
HOLD STILL.
OOF!
BLOODY HELL.

HMM. PLACE LOOKS FAMILIAR.
WHERE DID SILK DISAPPEAR TO?
HEY! NINJAK! CAN YOU HEAR ME?!
WELL, IF I HAD TO GUESS, I'D SAY THROUGH ONE OF THESE GAPING HOLES IN REALITY.
THAT'S WHAT I WAS AFRAID OF.
IT'S PUNK MAMBO! CAN YOU SEE ME?
I'M REALLY TIRED OF PORTALS.
GILAD...THIS... THIS IS THE UNDEAD MONK. THE ONE WHO TRAINED ME LONG AGO...BUT HE'S DIFFERENT NOW.
THE HELL YOU TALKING ABOUT, 'JAK?

YO, GUV! I DON'T HAVE LONG! YOU HEAR ME?! FOCUS!
MAMBO! I HAVEN'T SEEN YOU IN AGES! BUT YOU'RE STILL YOUNG. HOW IS THAT POSSIBLE?
THIS LOOKS LIKE SHANGRI-LA... THE UNDEAD MONK'S TEMPLE. IS HE BACK?
THE MONK IS NEVER REALLY GONE...
IT'S ALL COMING BACK NOW...
FZZZZZSHH
YOU'RE FROM THE PAST. FROM WHEN I HAD THAT DEADSIDE PARASITE.
I WAS TRYING OUT THE HYPER-MEDITATION I'D LEARNED FROM A MIND MASTER IN ZANZIBAR.
LIKE THE ULTIMATE ACID TRIP FLASHBACK.
LET'S ME INHABIT MY MEMORIES--WALK THROUGH THEM. LIVE THEM AGAIN.
COLIN? ARE YOU TALKING...TO YOURSELF?

SO WHAT HAPPENED THIS TIME?
I CAME BACK FROM OPERATION: DEADSIDE WITH A SUPER-NATURAL PATHOGEN IN MY BRAIN. THIS...THIS BUG EXISTS ACROSS ALL OF TIME AT ONCE. IN THE PAST AND NOW.
SO WHEN YOU HYPER-MEDITATED... YOU WERE ABLE TO RIDE THIS "BUG"...FORWARD THROUGH TIME?
MY CONSCIOUSNESS DID. AND IT ZEROED IN ON MY PRESENT. THERE MUST BE A REASON FOR THAT.
COLIN... WHO...WHAT ARE YOU TALKING ABOUT?
I THINK I'M GOING TO FIND THE CURE ON THE MISSION.
WELL, WHENEVER YOU'RE DOING PIGGY-BACKING YOUR FUTURE SELF, YOU'D BETTER GET BACK TO THE PRESENT. YOU'RE NOT LOOKIN' SO GOOD.
YOU OKAY TO CONTINUE? WE'VE GOT TO GO OR WE MAY LOSE SILK FOREVER.
HOLD ON. WE SHOULD WEAR THESE. PROTECT OURSELVES FROM DEADSIDE PATHOGENS.
NOT THAT YOU EVER DID.
COLIN?
WHAT?
HMM...LET'S SEE HOW REAL THIS ACID TRIP IS...
PFFOOOT!
WE'VE BEEN INOCULATED FROM THE DEADSIDE FOR YEARS.

WE HAVE? THERE'S A VACCINE?
YES.
YOU DEVELOPED IT.
...
COLIN'S SUBCONSCIOUS IS STRONG.
LIKE AN INTERACTIVE DREAM...
THAT MAKES SENSE...IF I SUCCEED HERE... I'D MAKE THE VACCINE BACK THEN.
INTERACTIVE... AND PERSISTENT. I CAN'T CHANGE WHAT'S HAPPENED.
NEITHER CAN HE. ALL HE CAN DO IS WATCH HIS FUTURE SELF AND SEE WHAT HE'S GOING TO DO.
IN THE SPIRIT OF EQUANIMITY, WHY DON'T YOU GO FIRST THIS TIME?
LET ME CLEAR MY HEAD FOR A SECOND. JUST FEELING A LITTLE FUZZY AROUND THE EDGES...
I'M A LITTLE WORRIED ABOUT YOU.
THE PARASITE IS EXISTING IN ALL TIMES AT ONCE. CREATING A WORMHOLE THROUGH ALL TIME.
NEVER SEEN ANYTHING LIKE THIS.
IF YOU'D PREFER TO STAY HERE, I'LL UNDERSTAND. YOU'LL GET FULL MARKS IN MY REPORT TO MI--
--WHAT THE?! AHHH!
MAMBO... COME BACK...
HUH? WHAT'S THA--
COME BACK...!
--WHAT THE BLOODY--

WH-WHERE IS THIS?
...CAN'T BREATHE...
...SO HUMID... FEEL LIKE WE'RE UNDERWATER...
KEEP GOING...
GHHHA!

SSSPLORRTCHSHH!
WELL, YOU'RE QUIET.
NO TALES FROM THE PAST THAT THIS REMINDS YOU OF?
ME NEITHER.
NOW WHERE?

THERE.
DID I EVER TELL YOU ABOUT THE SUMMER I SPENT WITH T. E. LAWRENCE?
NO.
WE'D BEEN CAMPING WITH THE BEDOUIN TRIBES WHEN--
NO, I MEANT DON'T TELL ME.

NGH!
COLIN?
S'OKAY. JUST KEEP GOING. I'LL CATCH UP.
YOU REMEMBER YEARS AGO? I HAD THAT BRAIN PARASITE FROM THE DEADSIDE?
WELL... APPARENTLY... THIS IS WHEN I FIND THE CURE FOR MY PAST SELF.
UH...YOU SURE YOU'RE GOING TO BE OKAY?
FORGET IT. LET'S GO.

UNBELIEVABLE. STRUCTURE MUST BE A KILOMETER HIGH AND MADE COMPLETELY OF WOOD. BUT NO FOREST IN SIGHT...
PLACE IS ABSOLUTELY DESOLATE...

YOU THINK THIS IS THE INTELLIGENCE MECHANISM THAT SILK WAS RAMBLING ON ABOUT?

HEADS UP!
WHAT?!
BOGEY, HIGH NOON.
HALT, INTERLOPERS.

FIRST RULE OF ESPIONAGE. ACT LIKE YOU BELONG.
WE'RE HERE TO ACCESS THE DEADSIDE INTELLIGENCE MECHANISM.
FOR WHAT PURPOSE?
WE HAVE REASON TO BELIEVE IT MAY BE THE TARGET OF AN IMPENDING ATTACK.
BY ALL ACCOUNTS, THIS TREASURE HOLDS INFINITE KNOWLEDGE. WHY WOULD YOU KEEP IT OUT HERE SO VULNERABLE AND UNPROTECTED?
A GOOD QUESTION. BUT AN EASY ONE.
WE KEEP IT OUT HERE...
SO ANY THREAT THAT APPROACHES CAN BE SEEN FROM MILES AWAY. AND I CAN ASSURE YOU...

...IT IS ANYTHING BUT UNPROTECTED.

WHAT? IT'S NOT MY FAULT?
KA-RUN-CH-A-H!
GILAD!
CRNNCH!
THAT WAS MY FRIEND, YOU SODDING, OVERGROWN CHERUBS.
YOU JUST MADE A BLOODY BIG MISTAKE.
TO BE CONCLUDED

KING'S CASTLE.
NOW.
THE LOST FILES
THE SITUATION IS THIS. COLIN CAME BACK FROM THE DEADSIDE ALONG WITH THE MI-6 SUPPORT AGENTS THAT HAD BEEN CAPTURED OVER THERE.
AFTER THEY RETURNED, THEY ALL CONTRACTED SOME KIND OF...VIRUS. AFFECTS THE MIND. IT'S ACTUALLY A LIVING VIRUS...INSIDE THEIR HEADS.
GOT IT. YOUR FAVORITE BLOKE'S GOT DEADSIDE BRAIN CANCER AND YOU WANT ME TO FIX IT.
LOOKS LIKE HE WENT INTO A TRANCE TO COPE WITH THE PARASITE. ONLY ONE WAY TO FIND OUT WHAT'S GOING ON IN THERE...

PUFF!
HMM.
WELL. YOU'RE GONNA HAVE TO PAY ME EXTRA FOR THIS, NEVILLE. POWDER NEEDS A JUMP START... ONLY WAY...
PSSTT SPPPST SPPST...

THAT'S MORE LIKE IT.
HEY! NINJAK! CAN YOU HEAR ME?!
WHERE DID SILK DISAPPEAR TO?
WELL, IF I HAD TO GUESS, I'D SAY THROUGH ONE OF THESE GAPING HOLES IN REALITY.
THAT'S WHAT I WAS AFRAID OF.
IT'S PUNK MAMBO! CAN YOU SEE ME?
I'M REALLY TIRED OF PORTALS.
GILAD...THIS... THIS IS THE UNDEAD MONK. THE ONE WHO TRAINED ME LONG AGO...BUT HE'S DIFFERENT NOW.
THE HELL YOU TALKING ABOUT, 'JAK?

YO, GUV! I DON'T HAVE LONG! YOU HEAR ME?! FOCUS!
MAMBO! I HAVEN'T SEEN YOU IN AGES! BUT YOU'RE STILL YOUNG. HOW IS THAT POSSIBLE?
THIS LOOKS LIKE SHANGRI-LA... THE UNDEAD MONK'S TEMPLE. IS HE BACK?
THE MONK IS NEVER REALLY GONE...
FZZZZZSHH
IT'S ALL COMING BACK NOW...
YOU'RE FROM THE PAST. FROM WHEN I HAD THAT DEADSIDE PARASITE.
I WAS TRYING OUT THE HYPER-MEDITATION I'D LEARNED FROM A *MIND MASTER* IN *ZANZIBAR.*
LIKE THE ULTIMATE ACID TRIP FLASHBACK.
LET'S ME INHABIT MY MEMORIES--WALK THROUGH THEM. LIVE THEM AGAIN.
SO THE 'JAK I'M WITH IS HAVING A MEMORY...OF THE FUTURE. THAT'S HOW I'M ABLE TO CONNECT WITH YOU THROUGH YOUR YOUNGER SELF.
COLIN? ARE YOU TALKING TO YOURSELF?

SO WHAT HAPPENED THIS TIME?
I CAME BACK FROM OPERATION: DEADSIDE WITH A SUPER-NATURAL PATHOGEN IN MY BRAIN. THIS...THIS BUG EXISTS ACROSS ALL OF TIME AT ONCE. IN THE PAST AND NOW.
MY CONSCIOUSNESS DID. AND IT ZEROED IN ON MY PRESENT. THERE MUST BE A REASON FOR THAT.
SO WHEN YOU HYPER-MEDITATED... YOU WERE ABLE TO RIDE THIS "BUG"...FORWARD THROUGH TIME?
COLIN... WHO...WHAT ARE YOU TALKING ABOUT?
I THINK I'M GOING TO FIND THE CURE ON THIS MISSION.
WELL, WHENEVER YOU'RE DOING PIGGY-BACKING YOUR FUTURE SELF, YOU'D BETTER GET BACK TO THE PRESENT. YOU'RE NOT LOOKIN' SO GOOD.
YOU OKAY TO CONTINUE? WE'VE GOT TO GO OR WE MAY LOSE SILK FOREVER.
NOT THAT YOU EVER DID.
HOLD ON. WE SHOULD WEAR THESE. PROTECT OURSELVES FROM DEADSIDE PATHOGENS.
COLIN?
WHAT?
HMM...LET'S SEE HOW REAL THIS ACID TRIP IS...
PFFOOOT!
WE'VE BEEN INOCULATED FROM THE DEADSIDE FOR YEARS.
WE HAVE? THERE'S A VACCINE?

YES.
YOU DEVELOPED IT.
...
COLIN'S SUBCONSCIOUS IS STRONG.
LIKE AN INTERACTIVE DREAM...
THAT MAKES SENSE...IF I SUCCEED HERE... I'D MAKE THE VACCINE BACK THEN.
INTERACTIVE... AND PERSISTENT. I CAN'T CHANGE WHAT'S HAPPENED.
NEITHER CAN HE. ALL HE CAN DO IS WATCH HIS FUTURE SELF AND SEE WHAT HE'S GOING TO DO.
IN THE SPIRIT OF EQUANIMITY, WHY DON'T YOU GO FIRST THIS TIME?
THE PARASITE IS EXISTING IN ALL TIMES AT ONCE. CREATING A WORMHOLE THROUGH ALL TIME.
NEVER SEEN ANYTHING LIKE THIS.
I'M A LITTLE WORRIED ABOUT YOU.
LET ME CLEAR MY HEAD FOR A SECOND. JUST FEELING A LITTLE FUZZY AROUND THE EDGES...
IF YOU'D PREFER TO STAY HERE, I'LL UNDERSTAND. YOU'LL GET FULL MARKS IN MY REPORT TO MI--
--WHAT THE?! AHHH!
MAMBO... COME BACK...
HUH? WHAT'S THA--
--WHAT THE BLOODY--
COME BACK...!

--COME BACK TO US!
--HELL?!
COUGH COUGH!
COUGH!
WHAT HAPPENED? DID YOU GET TO HIM? WHAT'S GOING ON?
WELL...

THE NUTTER'S GONE AND PUT HIMSELF IN A COMA TO SLOW DOWN HIS BODY. THAT BRAIN GRUB IS LIVING ACROSS TIME AND SPACE. IT'S GIVING HIM A KIND OF BRIDGE THROUGH TIME.
FROM WHAT I CAN TELL... HIS BODY'S HERE.
BUT HIS MIND?
'EE'S IN THE FUTURE.
TO BE CONCLUDED

MATT KINDT
KHARI EVANS
ORES GUINALDO
ERIC NGUYEN
LISES ARREOLA
RIS SOTOMAYOR
NINJAK
VALIANT
#21
THE FIST & THE STEEL

HE FUTURE.
N THE DEADSIDE.
THERE MUST BE SOME KIND OF MISUNDER-STANDING.
THERE'S NO MISUNDERSTANDING, INTERLOPER.
THAT'S JUST IT. ME AND MY FRIEND, GILAD? WE'RE FOLLOWING AN EVIL BLOKE NAMED SILK INTO YOUR REALM...BECAUSE HE'S GOT SOME SINISTER DESIGNS ON YOUR MAGICAL SUPERCOMPUTER--THE *DEADSIDE INTELLIGENCE MECHANISM.*
SO WHEN YOU KICK MY FRIEND A HUNDRED METERS INTO THE DESERT?
THERE HAS *DEFINITELY* BEEN A MISUNDER-STANDING.
YOU'RE EITHER GOING TO HELP US GET SILK OR...

NGGGHHA!
SHUKKKK!
...WELL, THERE IS NO "OR."
FWMP!
BRING IT ON, YOU STEROID CUPIDS.

GAH! MY EYES!
BAMFWOOOOOSSH!
I CAN'T SEE!
KILL THE INTERLOPER!
SWARM HIM!
SSHKKK!
SHKKK!
HKKK!
AGGGH!

WHERE DID HE GO?!
THERE!
HE'S ESCAPING!
THE HERETIC MUST PAY FOR HIS INSOLENCE!
HELLO?! WHERE IS EVERYONE?

NINJAK?
DID HE...REALLY RUN AWAY?
NO...
THE CUPIDS ARE CHASING MY MINIATURE AUTOMATED HOLO-SPHERE. A DECOY.
CLEVER. BUT NOW HOW DO WE GET IN? I HAVE A FEELING THEY WERE THE KEEPERS OF THE KEY TO GETTING IN TO THIS MONOLITH.

I DON'T SEVER LIMBS LIGHTLY.
THE KEY TO GET IN?
RIGHT HERE. MY CONTACT LENS SCANNER DETECTED IT WHEN THEY HAD US SURROUNDED.
ULTRAVIOLET SCAN SHOWS THE ENTRANCE SHOULD BE RIGHT...
BZZZZZ
...HERE.
SHCHUNK!
AFTER YOU.

HERE'S THE PLAN. YOU NEUTRALIZE SILK. I HAVE A...SIDE MISSION I NEED TO COMPLETE.
WHAT SIDE MISSION? THOUGHT I ASKED YOU TO HELP ME CAPTURE SILK?
YES, YES YOU DID. BUT MY, UH...MY PAST SELF HAS BEEN IN CONTACT WITH ME AND...WELL, IT'S A LONG STORY. LET'S JUST SAY I NEED TO RETRIEVE SOME CRITICAL INTEL FROM THIS MAGICAL SUPERCOMPUTER WHILE WE'RE HERE.
OKAY, THAT'S IT! WHAT THE HELL ARE YOU TALKING ABOUT? YOU'VE BEEN ON AND ON ABOUT THE PAST THIS ENTIRE MISSION! I FIGURED YOU'D JUST GONE SENILE BUT--
CLNK!
BZZ!
KRSSH!
WAIT! DO YOU HEAR SOMETHING--?

BZZ!
CLNK!
WHA?!
BZZ!
CLNK!
BZZZ!
CLNNK!
BZZZ!
SHKKK!
SOME KIND OF SENTRY BOTS TO KEEP INTRUDERS OUT.
BLAM! BLAM!
I'VE BEEN TREATED LIKE WORSE...
BZZZ!
DAMN THINGS KEEP ON COMING!
CLNNK!
BZZZ!
CRAK!
KRSSH!
SILK'S NOT IN SIGHT... WE NEED TO GET CLEAR OF THESE THINGS...
KRSSH!
I THINK THEY ARE REACTING TO YOUR HEAT SIGNATURE. SINCE MY SUIT HIDES MINE...
BZZZ!

...I'LL GET A HEAD START.
KRSSH!
GO! GET HIM!
BLAM! BLAM!
SOONER WE CAN GET OUT OF HERE, THE BETTER.
SHKKK!
I'LL MEET YOU UPSTAIRS!
DON'T TAKE TOO LONG.
I AM *NOT*... ~*HUFF*~--GETTING TOO OLD FOR THIS.
OH! *OH.* OH, BUGGER ME. THE HELL...?!

...NGHA... KNOWLEDGE...ALL THOUGHT...ALL TIME...THE DEADSIDE INTELLIGENCE MECHANISM...IS GOD... ANSWERING MY PRAYER... I--I'VE TAPPED THE VEIN OF ETERNAL LIFE...THE MAGIC...THE... HUHUH...UHNG...

THERE ARE JUST SOME SIGHTS...I WISH I'D NEVER SEEN.
MAINLINING THE MAGICAL KNOWLEDGE WITHIN THE INTELLIGENCE MECHANISM HAS KNOCKED SILK FOR A LOOP. HE'S REALLY OUT OF IT.
MAKES MY JOB EASY.
MISSION ACCOMPLI--
SHHZZZZZZT
WELL, THAT'S NOT GOOD. SILK'S GOT SOME KIND OF PROTECTIVE SPELL RUNNING THROUGH THE INTELLIGENCE MECHANISM. THE COMPUTER IS PROTECTING HIM.

I'LL HAVE TO HACK INTO IT TO GET TO HIM. FORTUNATELY... EVERY COMPUTER HAS A BACK DOOR...JUST NEED TO FIND...
A WAY...
...IN!
CRASH!

AMAZING.
BZZZZ
HITTER CHATCHITTER! CHITTER
NO WONDER THIS THING IS MILES HIGH. IT'S STORING VAST AMOUNTS OF KNOWLEDGE OF THE KNOWN AND UNKNOWN UNIVERSE... *MECHANICALLY.*
BZZZZ
HITTER CHAT ER! CHITTER
HITTER CHATCHITTER!
BZZZZ
ALL BRASS AND PAPER AND METAL. WHO...WHO THE BLOODY HELL BUILT THIS THING? AND HOW DO I HACK IT...?

THING IS RUNNING ON MAGIC AND STEAM...
BZZZZZ
BUT IT'S STILL RUNNING CODE...JUST NEED TO INTERPRET IT...
LEARN HOW TO SPEAK IT'S LANGUAGE...
CONTACT LENS VIDEO CAN SLOW THE CODE DOWN...LET ME DECIPHER IT...

JUST A MATTER OF PUSHING THE RIGHT BUTTONS AND PULLING THE RIGHT LEVERS.
SHK!
SHUNK!
SHUNKK!
SHUNK!
SHK!
SHK!
CODE TO RESTART THE SYSTEM SHOULD BREAK SILK'S SPELL AND--
SHUNKK!
AAAAAHGGG!

...OPEN ANOTHER PORTAL?!
DO YOU KNOW HOW MANY GENERATIONS I'VE BEEN WORKING ON THAT SPELL?
DO YOU KNOW HOW MANY FORTUNES I AMASSED AND LOST TO GAIN THE SECRET KNOWLEDGE? TO ACHIEVE IMMORTALITY?! I WAS SECONDS AWAY!
AND THEN YOU COME BARGING IN--! LIKE A CHILD BANGING ON A GRAND PIANO... RUINING EVERYTHING!
YOU DONE?
I'LL KILL YOU...AND THEN I'LL BE--!
SHUKKKK!

NO... NO!
ALLEY...
NO... WHAT ARE YOU--?!
...OOP!
AAAAAAAHHHHHHH!
I'LL BE DAMNED. THE PORTAL YOU OPENED UP WITH YOUR "COMPUTER HACK"... LOOKS A HELL OF A LOT LIKE...A PORTAL TO HELL.
HOW'D YOU DO THAT?

PROGRAMMING IS PROGRAMMING. THIS IS JUST A VERY DIFFERENT OPERATING SYSTEM. BUT HOLD THAT THOUGHT.
I HAVE A COUPLE QUESTIONS I NEED TO ASK THIS INTELLIGENCE MECHANISM BEFORE WE GO.
SINCE WE'RE HERE...
MIGHT AS WELL ASK THE GREAT OZ TO SOLVE A COUPLE MORE PROBLEMS...
SHNK!
BZZZZ
CHITTER CHATCHITTER! CHITTER CH

THERE MUST BE AN INFINITE AMOUNT OF CARDS AND DATA STORED IN THIS MONOLITH. MORE PROCESSING POWER THAN ALL THE MINDS ON EARTH...
BZZZZZ
AND I SWEAR IT'S...IT'S TALKING TO ME...
SWITCH!
SWITCH!
SWITCH!
BZZZZZ
DAMN THING'S SENTIENT...
SWITCH!
BZZZZZ
IT'S... IT'S IN MY HEAD...
BZZZZZ
READING MY THOUGHTS.
BZZZZZ

SHHHUNK!

COLIN?
YOU OKAY?
YOU GET THE ANSWERS YOU NEEDED?
LET'S GO.

LET ME GET THIS RIGHT. YOUR MEDITATING PAST SELF CONTACTED YOU HERE IN THE PRESENT?
HIS FUTURE. OUR PRESENT.
TO TELL YOUR FUTURE SELF--THE COLIN I'M TALKING TO NOW--TO TELL HIM THAT HE NEEDS TO GET A CURE FOR A DEADSIDE PARASITE?
THE PARASITE THAT YOU CURRENTLY DON'T HAVE.
I'M PRETTY SURE IT'S STILL IN MY HEAD...JUST NOT ACTIVE ANYMORE.
SO YOU SENT THIS CURE YOU JUST FOUND...TO THE PAST YOU...TO CURE YOURSELF.
I DIDN'T HAVE TO "SEND" IT. ONCE I KNEW IT...I ALWAYS KNEW IT.
...
YOU KNOW, YOU SHOULD TALK TO MY BROTHER, IVAR, THE TIMEWALKER.
PLEASE... YOU'RE THE ONLY ONE OF YOUR BROTHERS I CAN HALFWAY STAND.
I'VE ALWAYS RESPECTED YOUR WARRIOR MENTALITY, COLIN. I FEEL LIKE WE'VE REALLY FORMED A BOND...
UGH. PLEASE STOP TALKING.

PRESENT DAY.
UUHUH?!
HE'S AWAKE!
NGH!
FWUMP!

NGAAH... HUFF... I...
...I...
PLEASE... GIVE HIM SOME ROOM...AND GET A TRANSPORT. WE NEED TO GET HIM TO THE HOSPITAL!

THE NEXT DAY.
"I'M NOT SURE I UNDERSTAND EXACTLY WHAT YOU DID, NINJAK.
"ALL I KNOW IS THAT WE'VE GOT A SQUAD OF SPECIAL OPS THAT OWE THEIR LIVES TO YOU."
THE CURE TO THE BRAIN PARASITE? TRANGE RECIPE BUT UR LAB BOYS WERE ABLE TO MAKE IT.
SKIN FLAKES FROM YOUR OLD TEACHER, THE UNDEAD MONK?
ODD TO SAY THE LEAST. HERE'S AN EXTRA DOSE. MAYBE WE CAN DEVELOP A VACCINE FOR FUTURE DEADSIDE MISSIONS?

THANKS, NEVILLE.
COLIN... I'M SORRY MI-6...
I'M SORRY I COULDN'T HAVE DONE MORE TO HELP YOU.
YEAH.
IT'S MY FAULT. TRUSTING YOU? TRUSTING MI-6? WELL...

THIS IS WHAT I GET.

WE DESERVE THAT. WE'LL OWN IT. BUT I FEEL LIKE...SOMETHING HAPPENED THAT YOU'RE NOT TELLING ME. SOMETHING MORE.
I REPROGRAMMED THAT COMPUTER IN THE DEADSIDE. BUT I DID SOMETHING ELSE...
I SAW SOMETHING I *SHOULDN'T* HAVE. I *ASKED* IT A QUESTION I *DIDN'T* WANT THE ANSWER TO.
WHAT DID YOU ASK?
I ASKED AFTER ROKU... AFTER ANGELINA.
...
IT TOLD ME WHAT HAPPENED TO HER. WHAT... *HAPPENS* TO HER.
AND...?
ROKU... OR WHATEVER'S LEFT OF THE WOMAN I CARED ABOUT? ANGELINA? SHE *DIES*.
AND *I'M* THE ONE THAT *KILLS* HER.
END.

GALLERY

NINJAK #18 COVER B
Art by RYAN BODENHEIM
with MICHAEL GARLAND

NINJAK #19 COVER B
Art by DIEGO LATORRE

NINJAK #20 VARIANT COVER
Art by MICHEL FIFFE

NINJAK #21 VARIANT COVER
Art by JUAN JOSÉ RYP with GABE ELTAEB

NINJAK #18, p. 9
Art by KHARI EVANS

NINJAK #18, p. 11
Art by KHARI EVANS

NINJAK #18, p. 18
Art by KHARI EVANS

NINJAK #19, p. 18
Art by KHARI EVANS

NINJAK #19, p. 21
Art by KHARI EVANS

NINJAK #19, p. 22
Art by KHARI EVANS

NINJAK #20, p. 3
Art by KHARI EVANS

NINJAK #20, p. 19
Art by KHARI EVANS

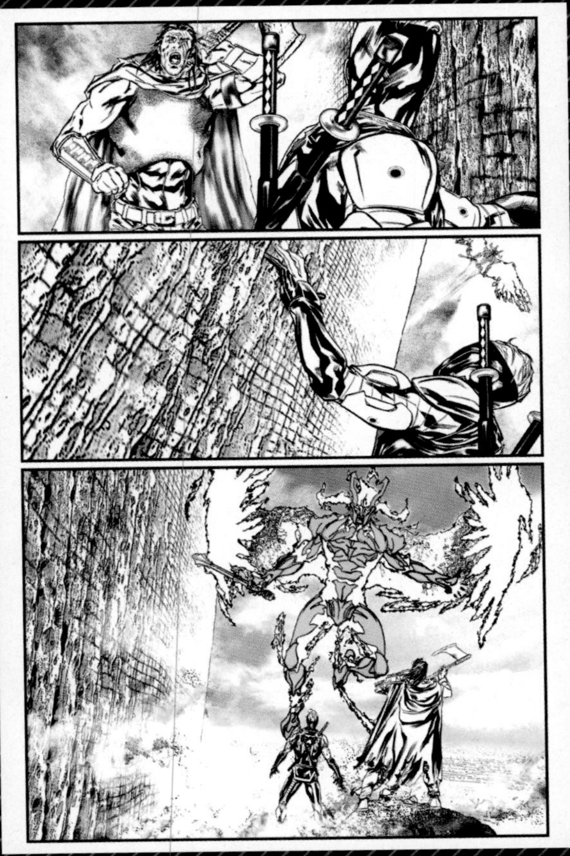

NINJAK #20, p. 21
Art by KHARI EVANS

EXPLORE THE VALIANT UNIVERSE

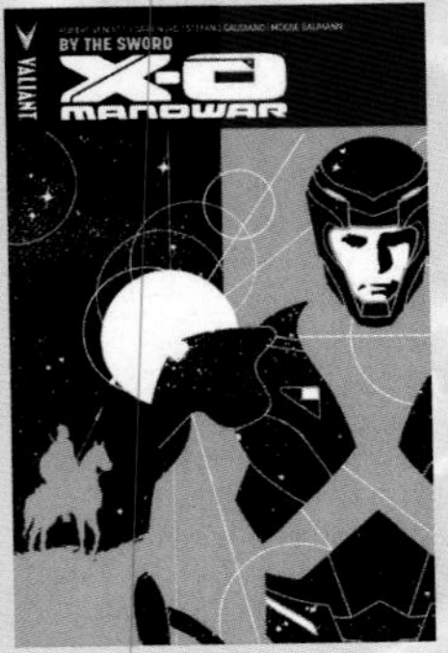

4001 A.D.

4001 A.D.
ISBN: 9781682151433

4001 A.D.: Beyond New Japan
ISBN: 9781682151464

Rai Vol 4: 4001 A.D.
ISBN: 9781682151471

A&A: THE ADVENTURES OF ARCHER AND ARMSTRONG

Volume 1: In the Bag
ISBN: 9781682151495

Volume 2: Romance and Road Trips
ISBN: 9781682151716

ARCHER & ARMSTRONG

Volume 1: The Michelangelo Code
ISBN: 9780979640988

Volume 2: Wrath of the Eternal Warrior
ISBN: 9781939346049

Volume 3: Far Faraway
ISBN: 9781939346148

Volume 4: Sect Civil War
ISBN: 9781939346254

Volume 5: Mission: Improbable
ISBN: 9781939346353

Volume 6: American Wasteland
ISBN: 9781939346421

Volume 7: The One Percent and Other Tales
ISBN: 9781939346537

ARMOR HUNTERS

Armor Hunters
ISBN: 9781939346452

Armor Hunters: Bloodshot
ISBN: 9781939346469

Armor Hunters: Harbinger
ISBN: 9781939346506

Unity Vol. 3: Armor Hunters
ISBN: 9781939346445

X-O Manowar Vol. 7: Armor Hunters
ISBN: 9781939346476

BLOODSHOT

Volume 1: Setting the World on Fire
ISBN: 9780979640964

Volume 2: The Rise and the Fall
ISBN: 9781939346032

Volume 3: Harbinger Wars
ISBN: 9781939346124

Volume 4: H.A.R.D. Corps
ISBN: 9781939346193

Volume 5: Get Some!
ISBN: 9781939346315

Volume 6: The Glitch and Other Tales
ISBN: 9781939346711

BLOODSHOT REBORN

Volume 1: Colorado
ISBN: 9781939346674

Volume 2: The Hunt
ISBN: 9781939346827

Volume 3: The Analog Man
ISBN: 9781682151334

Volume 4: Bloodshot Island
ISBN: 9781682151952

BOOK OF DEATH

Book of Death
ISBN: 9781939346971

Book of Death: The Fall of the Valiant Universe
ISBN: 9781939346988

DEAD DROP

ISBN: 9781939346858

THE DEATH-DEFYING DOCTOR MIRAGE

Volume 1
ISBN: 9781939346490

Volume 2: Second Lives
ISBN: 9781682151297

THE DELINQUENTS

ISBN: 9781939346513

DIVINITY

Volume 1
ISBN: 9781939346766

Volume 2
ISBN: 9781682151518

ETERNAL WARRIOR

Volume 1: Sword of the Wild
ISBN: 9781939346209

Volume 2: Eternal Emperor
ISBN: 9781939346292

Volume 3: Days of Steel
ISBN: 9781939346742

WRATH OF THE ETERNAL WARRIOR

Volume 1: Risen
ISBN: 9781682151235

Volumel 2: Labyrinth
ISBN: 9781682151594

FAITH

Faith Vol 1: Hollywood and Vine
ISBN: 9781682151402

Faith Vol 2: California Scheming
ISBN: 9781682151631

HARBINGER

Volume 1: Omega Rising
ISBN: 9780979640957

Volume 2: Renegades
ISBN: 9781939346025

Volume 3: Harbinger Wars
ISBN: 9781939346117

Volume 4: Perfect Day
ISBN: 9781939346155

Volume 5: Death of a Renegade
ISBN: 9781939346339

Volume 6: Omegas
ISBN: 9781939346384